LEAD GENERATION

21 Creative Ways to Generate Leads

SATISH GAIRE

Chapter Organization *by* Nikesh Chapagain

Book Interior *by* Pankaj Runthala

Cover & Mascot *by* /gangaiah

Fueled *by* Coffee & Mom's food

First Edition

Dedicated to those who supported me

(& especially those who didn't).

Labor Omnia Vincit

PREFACE

This book is slightly different from your typical marketing book. I don't fill chapters with useless text. I use bullet points instead. Business professors cringe when they hear my advice, because it is not "traditional" or "proper".

This book provides you with a crash course on lead generation. It then teaches you 21 powerful methods to use immediately to generate leads.

There are no fillers and there is no life story.

TABLE OF CONTENTS

CHAPTER 1

MECHANICS OF LEAD GENERATION

Generating leads is the life of any business. A company without a constant flow of leads in their pipeline, is as good as a closed business.

A lead generation campaign can be confusing because of the many business books that complicate the topic. They focus solely on components that can just be memorized and learned.

If you ask a MBA student, what "Lead generation" is, he/she will likely rephrase business books that were written in the 1990s. *Flash news: They don't work anymore.*

In order for you to stay ahead in the game of leads, you must eliminate the "standard" methods. This is because customers have gotten smarter and most of these techniques no longer work. You must be creative with your methods.

The "meat" of this book are the 30 channels that you can use to generate leads, the *Evil Salesman* way.

As a marketer, most of your time should be spent on the actual channels that bring leads, rather than things that you learn and master in a few hours. This book gives you a crash course on the foundation. However, the main focus will be on unique channels, where you can ACTUALLY generate leads.

The goal of this book is not to give you "ideas" on how you can generate leads. It will instead cover methods that have already been proven to work. You will notice that this book doesn't beat around the bush lengthen its chapters. It serves lead generation on a silver platter. *You are welcome!*

Just because I pointed out that the foundation is "not important," doesn't mean that you should skip it.

Marketers, before generating leads, must have four components in place: An Offer, Call To Action (CTA), Landing Page and Form.

CHAPTER 2

AN OFFER: SCARCITY

An offer is a piece of content that is perceived to be high in value. Offers include e-books, case studies, free consultations, coupons, exclusive demos etc.

In order for your offer to be attractive, it must have the following elements:

1. Use Scarcity in Your Offer

Scarcity means that when the supply is low in a certain timeframe, the demand goes up. This is the same reason why people kill each other for outdated items on Black Friday.

Humans want things with limited quantities because it means that the perceived value of the product is high.

There are three types of scarcity that can be used:

A. Limited time offers

You have likely been bombarded by emails which state that you can buy a pair of socks for 99 cents (which "normally" cost $99), if you buy within the vendor-specified timeframe.

In your offers, you should consider the following:

- Offer expires tonight at midnight
- Weekend ONLY special
- Add a timer on your campaigns
- Limited time bonus
- Early bird pricing
- Price increasing soon
- Holiday, special event offer
- Registration closing soon

Adding a timer on your offer boosts the conversion, because potential customers can actually visualize when the offer will end.

B. Limited quantity offers

The occurs when a vendor "limits" the quantity of product on the shelf, in order to create higher value. Your wife or girlfriend might not be happy when you tell this to her. However, this is exactly how the value of diamonds is regulated. There are a sufficient number of diamonds for everyone, but they release very small amounts of their stock to create a exclusively high value.

In your offers, consider following:

- Limited Seats Available

- Limited Quantity Available
- Only accepting 100 new students

Want to give your offer an even larger boost? Try using both elements in the offer. Groupon is an example of this technique. They have a limited number of items in stock, which must sell before Santa Claus leaves for the North Pole. Are you skeptical that people actually believe in this scarcity? Look at the lines at the Apple Store, when a new product is released. The consumer's brain is wired and triggered to get their credit card out, when they see the "Limited Offer."

Using scarcity is an easy way to drive more conversion, so use it.

CHAPTER 3

AN OFFER: HERD EFFECT

You go to a mall with a few of your friends. Two of them buy a shiny, cool watch that they saw on TV. You see another person buying the same watch.

What is your reaction? <u>Your brain will use flawed logic:</u>

"If two of my friends are getting this watch, it must be a trend and I must also get it, before I get left out "

This is called "Herd Effect." It is natural human behavior to copy another human being.

When possible, use numbers to indicate how many other people have joined, downloaded, purchased or enrolled in your offer.

- Join 18,300+ Customers Who Grew Their Business with Us
- Be part of Two Million+ Subscribers

Just make sure that your number is believable for the offer you are presenting. You cannot write things like "Join over Two Billion people who have joined our service"

Have you ever noticed testimonials at the bottom of sales pages or checkout pages? The vendor is using this same tactic.

It is recommended that you also include testimonials on your offer. Text testimonials work great, but video testimonials are better. Avoid buying testimonials from Fiverr because they are overused. Any smart consumer will figure this out quickly. It is better to get one of your friends or relatives to record the testimonial video for you.

The video does not need to be perfect. An amateur video is actually better. It looks more realistic. They can mumble a bit if necessary. It is okay.

CHAPTER 4

AN OFFER:
AVOID BUZZ WORDS

A "BuzzWord" is a fancy word that people use. They can usually be simplified into something that is clear and easy to understand, as shown in the table below:

Buzzwords "Sugar Coated"	Simple Version
Substantial	A lot
Sublime	Good
Due to the fact	Because
In the event of	If
Utilize	Use

Buzzwords actually make you sound fake. It is because they are sugar-coated versions of something simple.

Why do people use buzz words?

- To "appear" smart
- Lawyers use them to be vague and confusing
- Politicians use buzz words to sound important

- To promote an inferior product and make it seem valuable

- It is done by mistake and they do not realize that they are confusing their consumers

TDLR: Do not use buzzwords.

CHAPTER 5

AN OFFER: CREATE AMAZING TITLE

The title of your offer speaks for itself. Consumers will often skip the rest of the offer information and respond to the call to action (more on CTA later).

The title of your offer must be exciting:

- Get access to 45 unique channels to bring in new leads.
- Instant access to five tools to help you double your income.

It is important to notice that good titles make use of numbers. People respond to numbers. If you are having problems coming up with a good headline or title. I recommend this tool to get started. (https://www.aminstitute. com/headline/)

CHAPTER 6

AN OFFER: STAGES OF CONSUMERS

I have often seen marketers create ONE offer for everyone. This doesn't make sense, because each buyer is in a different stage of their buying cycle.

Salespeople and marketers frequently go straight for the close. This often does not work, because each person is in a different stage.

"Person A" might be in the research phase.

"Person B" might be in their comparison phase.

"Person C" might be in the ready to buy phase.

It is, therefore, very important that you create a different offer for each individual phase.

CHAPTER 7

AN OFFER: EXAMPLES OF HIGH CONVERTING OFFERS

You will love this chapter because I will list the types of offers that bring in the most leads. They are in the order of their performance:

- E-Books or guides
- Templates or presentations
- Research and reports (ex: State of Inbound Marketing)
- Whitepapers
- Kits (multiple offers packaged together)
- Live webinars
- On-demand videos
- Blogs (including offers in the nav or sidebar)
- Blog posts (if there is a CTA in the post)
- Middle-of-the-funnel offers: demo requests, contact sales.

CHAPTER 8

CALL TO ACTION

No matter how good of an offer you have, if you don't SPECIFICALLY ask people to do something, they won't.

Call to Action or CTA is an important element that will request people to do something.

CTAs can be used on landing pages, forms, emails, direct mails, etc.

You have likely seen this before. You get an email that tells you to "Click here to learn more." That is a CTA. You get a direct mail, that says "Call 1-800-Get-Rent to rent your home". That is also a CTA.

Many marketers create an amazing offer but forget to add a CTA or add a weak CTA, with no sense of URGENCY. (Scarcity) According to Small Biz Trends, 70% of small business B2B sites lack a call-to-action.

With Every CTA, you must review the following:

- **Clear Language:** Do you make it obvious about what you want done?

- **Design:** Does your CTA stand out? Does it have bright colors and good contrast?

- **Placement:** Is it placed where the user will see it easily?

- **A/B Testing:** Did you test multiple CTAs to see which performs better?

CHAPTER 9

CTA: PLACE THE CTA WHERE EYES CAN SEE IT

A rule of thumb on where to place your CTA, is on the "TOP FOLD" of the website. The top fold is a space that a user can see WITHOUT scrolling down the page.

It is also important to ensure that the colors for the CTA button are very bright and contrast with the actual website.

Some good colors to use are: red button with white text or a yellow button with black Text. They stand out and get the user's attention very easily.

For Example:

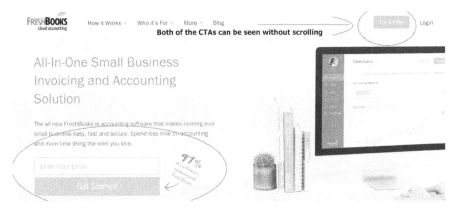

CTA: Place the CTA where eyes can see it

Make sure to also use this strategy for the mobile site.

CHAPTER 10

CTA: BENEFICIAL ORIENTED

Your CTA must somehow benefit your visitor. Otherwise, why would they waste their time clicking it and putting in their information?

Therefore, you have to clearly explain what they are getting in return.

Are they getting an e-book? access to a course or a free trial?

One of the easiest ways to convert your traffic, is to offer a free trial. If you think about it, no one wants to spend money the first time that they are on your website. This is especially true, if it's a recurring charge.

Our company has adopted a well-used tactic. We offer a free sample or a trial for a small amount. Does this ring a bell? "Try it for $1 a month, then $99 per month." You could also simply offer the first month for free.

Why should you offer a FREE trial?

You have already spent money running ads or took valuable time to get a visitor to the website. You need to get them in the "door". A free trial is an easy way to do that. How many times have you signed up for something to try it and are still paying for it? (I am also guilty of this)

Off-topic: Why do some companies charge $1? Does it really improve their revenue?

It is called "Smart Prospecting." They are making sure that the consumer has access to a credit card and you will be able to charge them instantly after the trial.

Any Tom, Dick or Harry will sign up for a free trial. However, if they are paying a dollar to see what it is, it means they actually got up, got their card and entered it.

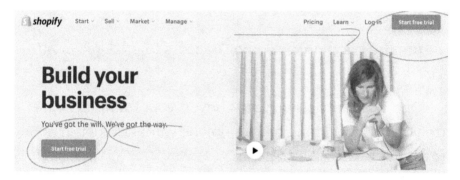

As you will notice on Shopify's home page, they follow the top fold rule. They use the "free trial" to increase their conversion.

CHAPTER 11

CTA: PLAY WITH THE EMOTIONS

As an EvilSalesman, you must be ruthless and be willing to play with and leverage the emotions of the consumer.

■ **Instant Gratification**

We want everything instantly, without getting out of our chair. It triggers our hypothalamus (Lord, my biochemistry degree actually proved useful).

When you promise something to the consumer, you must stick to it and give it to them. This will increase your conversion.

When writing your CTA, try to integrate these words into it.

- You

- Free

- Bonus

- Because

- Instant

- New

- **Urge to Belong**

  Humans are WIRED to belong somewhere. They want to be part of something that is bigger than them and to experience what others are experiencing.

  This is similar to the "Herd Effect". Therefore, you need to create a CTA where they can belong to a group of people who are experiencing the "RESULT" of taking an action.

  " Join 17,000+ customers, who have doubled their closing."

- **Agitate the problem, then offer a solution**

  This is a type of CTA where the marketer touts the problem and offers a solution, which is to take an action.

  Example:

  Are you tired of not getting women to talk to you? I know how it feels. Get access to a free eBook, where I share 40 ways to attract women. [Click Here]

  Some of you might be thinking, isn't this a "Beneficial-oriented CTA" ?

  Yes, it is. We evoked pain and gave them a solution.

At this point, many readers are making connections from the first part of the book. You are already noticing these things on websites, in malls and on billboards.

You got this!

CHAPTER 12

FORMS

Lead generation is not complete, without an actual form where people will enter their information or make a purchase.

We won't spend too much time on this chapter. It is clear on what you need to do, in order to increase your conversions.

- **Form Length**

    No one wants to fill out a long form. Make the form or checkout page, as short as possible. Grab the information that you need to be able to communicate with them.

    That information is usually their first name, email address and phone number.

As an example, if you are selling digital product, what is the point of collecting the shipping address and country? It is not necessary.

An example is one of our companies, DirectPay. On the checkout page, it asks for their name, email address and payment information. We will figure out the rest, once they have made the payment.

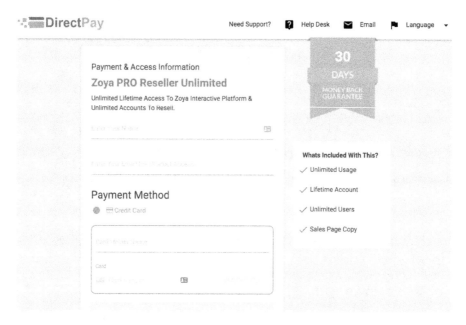

If you do have to collect a lot of information, make sure that you form looks shorter, by putting the fields closer together.

- Don't use "SUBMIT"

  When you use a form creator, the default button will probably say "SUBMIT." When you think about it, do you want to submit anything?

  You should instead turn it into a benefit. Some good examples are: Get a Free E-book, Join Newsletter or Start Making Money, etc.

- Provide reassurance

  In this age, when everyone is getting hacked, no one wants to submit their personal details on a random website. However, you can make it easier for them, by making a few changes.

  - Install SSL on your domain (such as https://) Ask your host.
  - If you belong to any organization like BBB, use their logo
  - Consider adding testimonials of past clients
  - Add security seals from your SSL
  - Add Privacy and Terms of Service Links at the bottom of your site.

CHAPTER 13

PERFECT LANDING PAGE

The landing page is where it all comes together. This is where all the action happens.

At this point, you are probably wondering, "What is a perfect landing page formula?"

You already know it (if you didn't skip last 12 chapters).

However, we need to get few things out of the way, so we are all on the same page.

- The landing page is not your normal home page.
- The landing page is separate from your company site.
- The landing page should not have navigation, in order to avoid distraction.
- The landing page has ONLY 1 goal.
- The more landing pages = more results
- The same landing page doesn't work for everyone.
- Landing pages get outdated as consumers change.
- The CTA must be displayed multiple times
- Avoid company philosophy and extraneous information

- Only collect the information that you need (as an example, get the zip code and skip the city and state).

- Make sure that you state the problem and how the CTA is solving the issue.

- Test several headlines

- Make sure that the landing page is mobile optimized.

- Skip the animation and exploding graphics. This is not the fourth grade.

- Make sure that the landing page loads in UNDER TWO SECONDS.

- Don't forget the testimonial/social proof.

STRONG AUTOMOTIVE MERCHANDISING

BASIC ANATOMY
OF A LANDING PAGE

[MANDATORY]

HEADLINE
Strong Headline that reinforces informational scent

IMAGERY
Compelling image to direct attention or convey a message

STRONG
AUTOMOTIVE MERCHANDISING

CTA
Clear Call to Action (Request for Information or Click Through)

SUB-HEAD
Secondary Headline

VALUE
Copy describing the value, features and benefits of your products and services

TRUST
Supportive Trust factors – Testimonial or Ratings

[ABOVE THE FOLD]

BELOW THE FOLD

ADDITIONAL INFORMATION
If you have more information to share or you want to provide more information, place the following below the fold.

VIDEO
Descriptive or How to Video

BENEFITS
Detailed Feature Benefit Copy

REPEAT CTA
Repeat the CTA

TRUST
Additional Trust Statements

NEW CTA
New CTA based on potential buying phase options (research, information, purchase)

OPTIONAL

DRIVING TRAFFIC SINCE 1977.

STRONGAUTOMOTIVE.COM

- Headline

  This is what we call the attention grabber. This will get people to read rest of your landing page.

  Consider using numbers and instant gratification.

  An example is: Every website owner needs this tool to boost their sales.

- Sub-Headline

  This is optional. However, it could actually help. Use sub-headlines, when it can complement your headline.

An example is: I am selling a software product that will help website visitors send voicemail directly via the website.

My headline could be: "Every website owner needs this tool to boost their sales."

Under it in a smaller font, I could put: "Cloud Based Voicemail Platform"

I must actually prove my headline. That can be done through testimonials, screenshots, video proofs, etc. However, the sub-headline lets your visitor know EXACTLY what you are offering.

- Video/Image

  You need to compliment your landing page with a relevant image or video. Many marketers make the mistake by putting in images that have nothing to do with the offer.

PRO TIP- When in doubt about image, use images of women and children. This is because both men and women love to look at women's pictures. Make sure that the image is not obscene, unless that is your target (dating leadgen!.

If you are selling insurance or any security product, be sure to include pictures of families or children. This triggers consumers to think about their own families.

If you are adding video, it should be under five minutes long. This is because people will generally not pay attention after that. The video must be creative, so that it holds the consumer's attention.

- Call to Action

It is important to remember the rule of putting CTA on the FIRST fold of the website, flyer etc. You should also put it at the end of the offer, because you want them to take an action after they have finished reading your offer.

PRO TIP: On our ecommerce website, we add "Add To Cart" as a floating button. Therefore, wherever they are on the screen. the button is right there.

- **Value Selling**

  On your landing page, you should make it clear to them exactly what they are receiving in exchange for their information or money.

  You must give them what you promised. That is as simple as it gets. If you promise your visitors access to 50 video modules, there had better be 51. It's always better to over deliver than under deliver.

  You should always focus on VALUE selling. Many companies focus on FEATURE selling. It doesn't work! Sell on the VALUE of having that feature.

  The value could be saving time, saving money, adding more revenue or a shortcut.

- **Second CTA**

  The second CTA should be at the bottom of the page or on the backside of the flyer, once they have actually read your offer.

34

You need to tell your consumer what you want them to do and then again remind them what they need to be doing.

- ■ Trust factors

No one wants to work with people who are not credible and they don't want to enter information at a random site they found.

Therefore, how do you increase the trust factor?

- Install a SSL certificate.
- Add Privacy and Terms of Service links at the bottom of the page (use very small fonts, since you don't want this to cause distractions).
- Use badges, such as BBB.
- Testimonials
- Use toll free 1-800 or 1-888 numbers on a Flyer or put them at bottom of site.
- Add "live chat," "offline messaging" or a support link.
- Offer refund policy, if this is a sales landing page

The goal is to reassure them that they are in good hands.

CHAPTER 14

PROMOTING CHANNELS

Once you have completed the basics and have a landing page with an offer to start, it is time to actually collect leads. We will now focus on WHERE and HOW to use the offer that you have created, to bring in more traffic and to convert visitors.

If you implement at least 10% of the mentioned channels, you will get results that you can actually see. This is the part of the book where people get lazy drop it.

Anything that is worthwhile in life, including lead generation, takes hard work. Fortunately for you, I have already used all of the following channels. I will give you tips and tactics that will lead to a successful campaign.

The next chapter should be used like a buffet. You can read what you feel interested in and skip topics, if you like. However, we offer insights on channels that you may already know about.

It will be helpful to read all of the promotion channels. You will notice that the chapters are very short and direct. There are no fillers.

CHAPTER 15

QUORA

Quora is like "Yahoo Answers". However, it is a hundred times better. People are asking for help and they expect experts to respond. Many people don't even know that they can generate leads here.

If you search for a response to a question on Google, it is likely that there will be a Quora answer on the top fold. This could be you.

- Responding to questions on Quora

  The first thing that you need to do, is to create your profile and to add all of your bragging points on your profile.

Satish Gaire

Founder of DirectPay, WooAgents , Podmio & 700+ Other SaaS

This page is a GOLDMINE.. Take GOOD 5 minutes and go over it.
You will not regret it.

Don't Forget To Subscribe To My " 1,000 Ways To Make Money " Series On YouTube. View Now

I am super active on Instagram, Follow Me:
https://www.instagram.com/sgaire/

——-

You can SKIP MBA if you watch this guy's Free Course

Finding Your First Million Dollar Idea
— ————-

Want FREEBIE Softwares? Free WordPress Plugins? Sales Page Builder? Checkout the link below:

GreatSteals - Freebies For Entrepreneurs

Follow Me On YouTube -Satish Gaire

What do i do for living?
- I run few hundred SaaS applications & I launch 7 figure software launches every week & i do bunch of other stuff that will probably bore you.

—My Fav Books—

Compressed Business Book Summaries

I then want you to go to the top search bar. You should then search for your topic or find questions that your ideal customers would have.

How easy is it to make money with a podcast?

Satish Gaire, Podcast Success Officer at Podmio.com (2016-present)
Answered Apr 16

Short Answer: It's Extremely Easy , Grab this free Monetization course.
Podcast Monetization Course - PodValley

The goal is to provide value. If you do that, people will come to you.

These suggestions for your answer will allow you to get more views/upvotes and make it go to top:

- Respond with a LONG answer, a short answer will not work.

- Add as many images/videos as possible.

- Have a friend or create a second Quora account and upvote yourself. This will elevate you to the top faster (yes, I will give you mobster-style suggestions).

- Write a question and post it from another account. You should then answer it.

- Quora Ads

  Many people don't realize that Quora also has an ads platform. Quora is actually inexpensive to run ads. They are very targeted, because people reading the questions/answers are already interested in that topic.

  Go to https://www.quora.com/business and register. There is nothing special to be done. You should make sure to run ads, for as little as $2 a day. You will see guaranteed results.

CHAPTER 16

INDEED.COM

This is a unique site. Indeed is a site where you can post job ads for free. The goal is to get creative to get many HOT leads.

As an example, if you sell cold calling courses, you would post a job that says cold callers wanted. You will notice that within hours, you will receive hundreds of applications. They will include their email address and personal cell number.

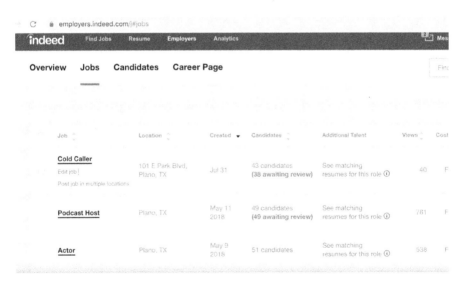

You can export this information into a .CSV. If you do a mass SMS, (Mass TEXT), you will instantly reach their phone.

You tell them that you are reaching out to see if they would be interested in taking your cold call course, which could certify them to get them the job of their dreams.

You might be thinking, will this work for me? Yes, but you have to be creative with your job posting.

We own a podcasting platform. We posted a job for podcast host. Guess what they need, if they are a podcast host? They need our software.

At this point, you might be thinking whether this book is going to turn me into a scammer. You are providing a course And they are getting something. Therefore, this is not scam. This is called the Evil Salesman lead generation system.

CHAPTER 17

PPC ADS FOR FACEBOOK AND IG

I am not going to teach you how to run ads. You can learn that from YouTube. I will teach you how to hustle to get more leads for the cheapest price.

I normally don't run Google Ads, unless a client needs local leads. This is because Google Ads is VERY expensive and it might not work, if you have a limited budget. It is not really worth it, if you are just capturing raw leads.

The following are some pointers about Facebook and Instagram ads.

- **Facebook Ads**
  - Run ads between 11 pm to 6 am penny clicks.
  - Automatic bidding is for dummies. You should manually enter the amount and then scale up.
  - Using pictures of sexy girls will get you more clicks.
  - People who don't re-target, are wasting their money.

- Default Placement ads will burn money. It is much better to pick and choose

- The focus should be on mobile content first.

- Video ads brings more conversions than images.

- Export some of your leads and enter them to a custom audience.

- Look-alike audience from your existing leads

- You should optimize behavior, job titles and income.

■ **Instagram Ads**

- Do not waste money on "STORY" ads.

- Run ads with a post under 40 seconds.

- The CTA should be your landing page, not your profile or DM.

- Run contest ads to increase your number of followers.

- You need to at least have 1,000 followers, before you can start giving advice.

- You should respond to both your fans and haters. This increases the engagement rate.

- It is important to use every chance you get to increase followers.

- Please follow @sgaire for other great tips.

sgaire ∨

88
Posts

52.9K
Followers

414
Following

Satish Gaire
Entrepreneur
Founder @ DirectPay/Podmio/WooAgents
NextWebinar Host
UNT: Biochemistry 🏠
Top Affiliate Marketer... more
www.sgaire.com/about/

CHAPTER 18

EMAIL SIGNATURES

How many emails do you send each week? I send out many emails and my team responds to even more. We, therefore, used our email signature to make people opt in.

Before you realize it, you will have many people who opted in to receive your marketing and promotional emails. I actually even highlight the CTA.

New Message

Recipients

Subject

--
Thank You
Satish Gaire
Cell (972) 363-4457

To receive weekly freebies, Please go there https://greatsteals.com/free

101 E Park Blvd 467
Plano, 75068

Office (469) 609-6479

https://www.linkedin.com/in/satishgaire/

CHAPTER 19

LINKEDIN

We all know what LinkedIn is, so I will skip the intro and get to the point. LinkedIn has professionals who are ready to buy.

- **Getting Email Leads**

    LinkedIn used to have a "hidden" feature to export your connections' personal email. That feature is now disabled. However, you can still get your connections' personal emails.

The step is to use the SEARCH bar to find people who you think might be beneficial for you. This could include categories such as dentist, writer or self-employed.

If you add them up you will find that there are many of them.

You then need to go to Upwork.com and post a job for an assistant, who will go through each of your contacts and manually collect your connections information. This shouldn't cost you more than $5 per hour. Hire Indians!

Once you have hired them, you will need to give them access to your LinkedIn. You should then ask them to go to all the recently added connections contact information to take their email and to put it in an excel sheet.

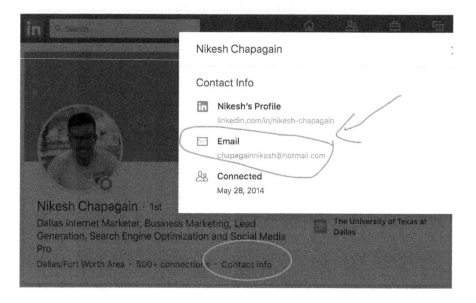

■ **Write Recommendations**

Write recommendations for the people who are on the top of the fields that you are targeting. It is likely that your lead will end up on their profile. They will see your recommendation, which will lead them to your profile. It is important to make sure that your profile is well set up.

For more help, visit https://HackThatLinkedin.com

- **LinkedIn Ads**

   LinkedIn ads are not cheap. However, they have one feature that is worth every penny. It allows you to send ads directly to your prospect's Inbox.

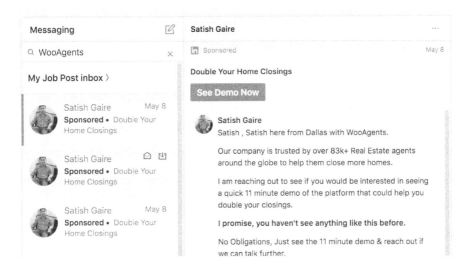

   These kinds of ads cost about 1-2 dollars per message. However, they end up in your target's inbox with the push of a button. I instantly sent out 100 messages for about $200. A total of 22 people responded and nine bought the platform worth $499 pm. It was completely worth the investment.

   Don't bother running other kinds of ads. They are very expensive and not worth it.

- **Pulse Articles**

   Pulse articles is just a blog on LinkedIn. The content ranks very well on Google. I encourage you to write a few articles.

CHAPTER 20

PODCASTING

I am sure that you know what Podcasting is. You need to create a Podcast with a company called Podmio.com Why should you use this company? It is because no other company offers the same type of lead generation features that they do.

- **Interview Someone**

    Once you create your Podcast, you need to interview someone who is well-respected in your industry. They will most likely agree to be on your show.

    Prior to interview, ask them if they can share the podcast on their social media etc. Even if you don't ask, it is likely that they will. People love to toot their horn, when they have been given the honor of an interview.

Here is the Evil part:

Podmio.com offers a podcast player that lets you capture leads directly from your episodes.

This is will help you to bring in leads from the person that you interview and other listeners who find the podcast through organic searches.

CHAPTER 21

LIVE CHAT

O n all of my landing pages, I have added "Live Chat", as a trust factor. However, it is also as a lead generation tool.

When people have important questions about your offer, they will ask questions and you can use this opportunity to collect their information.

Once you have their information, you can send them occasional information about your products. I recommend TWAK and TIDIO LiveChat services, which have free plans.

Things to keep in mind while choosing Live Chat Platform

- Supports Lead Capture.

- Has an iOS/Android App.

- Reputable company.

- Supports FB Bot (Optional).

CHAPTER 22

SOCIAL SHARING

With social sharing, you add a small code on your landing page. This allows other people to share the landing page on their social media pages.

If you send PPC traffic to your landing page and someone likes your offer and shares it on their social media, you will get more bang for your buck. However, you have to make it easy for them to share.

You can use services, such as "ShareThis" , "Image Sharer", "Shareaholic".

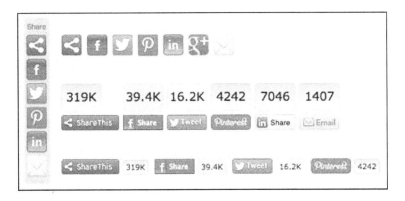

CHAPTER 23

GOOGLE PLACES BLACKHAT

If your company is collecting leads for local business, a neat trick that you can use to drive high volumes of leads is Google Places.

Google Places lets you add your business on Google Maps. However, they require address verification. People normally just have one entry with the name of their company. This situation requires you to get a little creative.

Dry Cleaning Service

Website Directions Save

3.5 ★★★☆ ☆ 8 Google reviews

Corporate office

Address: 467, 101 E Park Blvd, Plano, TX 75074

This "trick" works under the assumption that consumers will search Google for the actual service. Some examples could include a dry cleaning service or a roof repair company.

If you this method, you will rank at the top of Google Places for important keywords, without having to pay Google.

- **Register DBA Business Names**

   You can go to your local county clerk's office and ask to register a DBA (Doing Business As). You can register the company name "Dry cleaning Service" in every city. This will cost you about $10 each.

- **Get virtual address**

   One of the Google Places requirements is that you have to verify the address. Since you won't be buying 10 offices in 10 different cities, you need to visit UPS in each city and ask for a small mailbox. This costs about $20 every six months. They will give you a REAL address, and not P.O. Box #.

- **Create Google Places in each city**

   You can do this from the Google Places website. After you have done this, whenever people search for that service, the phone number and website for your company will be shown.

CHAPTER 24

B2B DATABASES

There are companies that sell b2b leads. However, access to these leads is very expensive. Many marketers spend thousands of dollars collecting these manually, when all they have to do is purchase them.

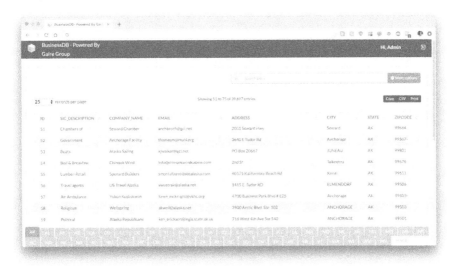

Here are two that I recommend:

- **US Biz Database (NextWebinar.org/go/getbizleads)**

  This service charges you a one-time $49 fee, which gives you access to the entire U.S. b2b database. The only drawback is that they are not updated daily. However, for $49, it doesn't get any better.

- **Zoom Info (ZoomInfo.com)**

  ZoomInfo charges you PER lead. This can get pretty expensive. However, the advantage of this resource is that the leads are updated weekly. Therefore, you are getting the latest information. This can be used for direct mailing.

CHAPTER 25

RANK YOUTUBE VIDEOS

YouTube videos are a great lead generation tool, because it ranks very well for organic searches.

The first step is to have a video created. This is a snapshot of your offer. It then involves gaming the system to rank on Google's Page #1 within hours.

This works very well for local business lead generation. If there was a hailstorm in Dallas, TX, everyone would be searching this on Google. As a result, Google adwords would skyrocket. However, there is a cheaper and almost free method.

- **Video Title**

    The video title needs to what people would search for. An example would be Roof replacement Dallas, TX. Make sure to include the main keyword and the city, if there is one.

- **Transcription**

    You need to transcribe your video. YouTube does this for free and creates Closed Caption.

- **Keywords**

  When uploading video on YouTube, there will be an option to enter keywords. Make sure to enter keywords that describe what you are offering.

- **Description/CTA**

  Your Description should have lots of information, including the CTA link to your offer/landing page.

- **Spend $50 on Ads**

  You need to run ads and spend about $50. It is recommended that you run google adwords ads with a limitation of $50 for the city you are targeting. This will help the ranking of your video, because it needs to have some views.

That is it. Within hours, your video should rank for keywords on Google's front page. *Caution: Unless you keep sending some traffic every week, the video will fall off. This is a method for local business to bring in extra leads their way.*

CHAPTER 26

QUIZZES & CONTESTS

Believe it or not, people love to take quizzes to find out the answers. For example, take this quiz to find out your business' weakness.

People also love to take quizzes, to see if they can win something. Everyone loves a chance to win free things.

It makes it interactive and fun when people respond to your offer. While they are taking the quiz, they will need to enter their information in order to get the results.

- You can find Quiz/Contest WordPress Plugins for Free
- Ask curious questions
- Offer to provide lucrative results via Email
- Ask for their name, email and phone number

Once your quiz is ready, you can promote it via PPC for the best and fastest results.

CHAPTER 27

GOING VIRAL ON REDDIT

Reddit allows you to take your lead generation to level that you would have never imagined.

When you go viral on Reddit, you will receive such a large volume of traffic, that your hosting company will trigger a DDOS. Therefore, you should be prepared (although AWS load balancers help).

- **Content Formula**

    You will need to make a post on one of their "Subreddits," which is a sub-forum. The content needs to actually provide real value.

    Reddit users LOVE a good STORY. A rags to riches story is guaranteed to mess with someone's mind to win their emotions. You should include several pictures. If you have children, use their pictures. Your English doesn't have to be perfect. If you make little mistakes, it seems more real.

■ Do it for the Votes

Upvote is like "LIKES" on reddit. They actually have a "Down Vote." Therefore, the idea is to balance them, so that you have at least 500 up votes.

Is this doable? Yes. Ask a few of your friends to upvote on the first day. Wait a few days and then get on Fiverr. com and Upwork.com to hire an agency for under $400 to bring in more upvotes.

Is $400 expensive? One of my clients wanted their content to go viral. She paid us almost $40,000 for content and 2000 upvotes. In return, she made all of her money back in the first week. She is still milking that content and is making a few thousand dollars each month.

CHAPTER 28

WEBINARS & WORKSHOPS

Webinars are similar to "Seminars," except they are done on the web. They are normally done "live" or at least simulated, if it is the same webinar every day.

The following is a good webinar format:

- Good introduction
- Give a snapshot of what's happening in the webinar, like an agenda.
- Have attendees get involved in the live session.
- Give something of value that you "normally" charge for.
- Have past testimonials participate in the call.
- Ask for the close, which could be buying something.

I intend to write an entire book on this topic in future, because there is so much to teach you. However, the scope of this book is limited to just lead generation.

The idea is that people love "Live Events". Therefore, you create a free webinar event once a month or every day, if you want to use a simulation.

Many new marketers stay away from this lead generation, because they are too shy to actually get their face in front of audience. The audience doesn't really care how you look, as long as you don't show up unprepared. Just have a good content and provide value.

- Nothing beats GoToWebinar for Webinars, but it is not cheap.
- On the cheaper end, Zoom is pretty good.
- The webinar could be your actual offer.

Workshops are the same thing but are usually done in a face to face format. However, they can also be done via webinar. This is your chance to teach something about which you are an expert to your potential customer, in order to gain their trust and to increase your credibility.

CHAPTER 29

TOOLS OF THE TRADE

If you were a mechanic and someone handed you a box of tools to fix cars as a gift, wouldn't you forever be in debt to that person? Would you think of them every time you used the tools? The idea of offering free tools as a lead manager, has a long-lasting effect in creating loyal fans and customers.

In every industry, there are tools that people use to collect leads. In banking, there is the mortgage calculator. Marketing has analyzers.

These tools are great way to generate leads.

For example, when I sold SEO software in 2014, I created a tool that would analyze a website's SEO and provide a report. On the backend, I scanned their WHOIS to grab their information.

If I couldn't grab their details, it would be asked when they downloaded the report in the PDF form.

CHAPTER 30

VIDEO OUTROS

If you are using YouTube for hosting your lead generation video, you could actually be losing many potential clients.

YouTube is not meant for businesses or marketing. Therefore, they don't offer analytics or features to help you grow your business.

I recommend Wistia or Vimeo, which both offer Outro lead capture form at the end of the video. By adding this form, you should be able to easily boost your lead generation by almost 5%.

CHAPTER 31

BUYSELLADS.COM

BuySellAds is a hidden gem that no one talks about. That is because everyone is busy reaping the benefits, including our company.

This site allows you to buy ad space on popular and not so popular websites directly from the vendor. This is instead of Google Adwords, where you must pay $50 a click and the website owner only receives a small amount.

You must first go to categories that best match your industry. You will then see a list of websites that are working directly in the marketplace to allow you to run ads on their site. This has proven to work very well for us. It allows us to run an ad on a website that we know can bring us fresh and quality leads.

CHAPTER 32

TEXT TO KEYWORD

The text to keyword method can be used on direct mail, websites and social media. This is a great method to let people opt in to your list, by texting to a keyword. This method allows you to reach out to them INSTANTLY on their phone via mass text.

We set up the cover of our Facebook group as a CTA to encourage people to text "Deals" to our number, so they could be notified to receive texts for our latest offers.

The result was that we had over 6,000 people sign up overnight, because they didn't want to miss out, when we were running special offers.

You can also use the same method for direct mail. This was done by using a software called MySMSBot. A link to this software can be found on EvilSalesman.com/tools/

The cost to use this software is very affordable. There is a $99 one-time fee and then it costs $0.00075 per text with your own personalized phone number.

CHAPTER 33

FREE CONSULTATIONS AND FREEMIUM

Free consultation and Freemium are classic methods of getting people to come to talk to you. There is free consultation in just about every industry.

The concept is that you get people to come talk to you or try your services for minimal or free price. You then you upsell them on other things that they may or may not need.

Every industry uses this model. Why do you think that dental exams or annual exams are either free or low-cost, even without insurance? Why do you think auto service businesses have the lowest margins on an oil change? This is an opportunity to get consumers to try the service or to convince them on upsells.

CHAPTER 34

MEETUP.COM

No. No. Meetup is not a dating website (well I guess it could be). Meetup is a place where you can create a group, based on your targets. Those who are interested, will receive an email from Meetup asking them to join.

This works very well, because Meetup charges about $100 every six months to create these groups. If no one joins the group, you can cancel the payment. Therefore, they send out emails to people who may be interested in joining your group.

Once you have created the group and you have members, you can run webinars for them, send them mass emails and collect their information. If the lead generation stalls, you can cancel the group, since you have all of their information to move forward.

CHAPTER 35

ACCESS123

Access123 is a tool that can be used as lead magnets to provide e-books, downloads and white pages, by letting you create a store front for free or even paid products.

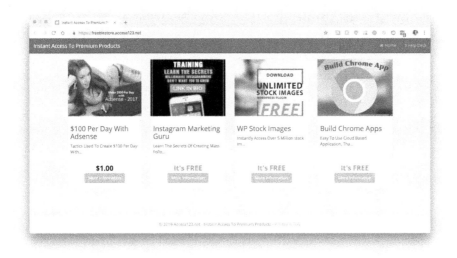

The reason Access123 works so well, is because it offers multiple lead magnets on one page. To the consumer, it feels like they are going to a candy shop and wanting everything that they see. In order for them to get the freebie, they must enter their information. Everything is then sent to their email, which ensures that the email is valid.

Making Money With Website Checklist

About Making Money With Website
Checklist

This is the checklist for making money online with a website. Learn how to turn $5 into $5,000!

GET IT NOW It's FREE

I have often run PPC ad campaigns with a link to this system, which has resulted in a large amount of lead generation.

If you don't have something to offer, you can find content on YouTube and then use it as an access URL, after they have opted in.

You could even charge a dollar or other small amount for a product to validate that the consumer has the ability to make a payment.

CHAPTER 36

WHAT'S NEXT

Generating leads is an art that takes time to master. As you try the methods that I have outlined, you will likely find something creative of your own.

Where do you go from here?

- **Keep up with learning via EvilSalesman.com**

  Lead generation is always changing and I would like to get the latest information to you via our website. It is 100% FREE.

- **Use on Existing campaigns**

  You can try these methods on your existing campaigns to instantly help you increase your conversion. Putting it to actual use is a great way to master it.

- **Become a consultant**

  You have the basic and crash knowledge to actually help others who may need help with lead generation. You can use what you have learned, add your own style to it and monetize it.

What's Next

Whatever you choose to do, my best wishes are with you. See you on the next book.

ABOUT THE AUTHOR

Satish Gaire is an internet marketer and entrepreneur. He is known as the "King of SaaS" platforms in the industry. In his 10-year career, he has launched over 700+ software products online. These softwares has helped millions of people worldwide operate and expand their business.

 : **@sgaire**

 : **/gairesatish**

 : **SatishGaire.com & EvilSalesman.com**